# TABLE OF CONTENTS

Table of Contents

Copyright

Note from the Author

Acknowledgements

Colleagues

Mentors

How to use this book

Chapter 1: SAP Legacy System Migration Workbench (LSMW) Overview

Chapter 2: Three steps to follow to make a successful LSMW

    Know the task at hand!

    Create LSMW

    Test your LSMW

Chapter 3: Overview of what we are doing – Knowing the task at hand.

    The Scenario

Chapter 4: Creating our first LSMW

    Step 1 – Accessing LSMW and the LSMW Initial Screen

    Step 2 – What is this all about: Project, Subproject and Object

    Step 2.1 – Create an LSMW Project

    Step 2.2 – Create an LSMW Subproject

Step 2.3 – Create an LSMW Object

Step 3 – Let's create our first Recording

Step 3.1 – Download the recording

Step 3.2 – Preparation for fast tracking later steps

Step 3.3 – Creating & Populating your template

Step 4 – Putting it together

Step 4.1 – Maintain object attributes

Step 4.2 – Maintain source structures

Step 4.3 – Maintain source fields

Step 4.4 – Maintain structure relations

Step 4.5 – Maintain field mapping and conversion rules

Step 4.6 – Quick overview of Fixed Values, translations and user-defined routines

Step 4.7 – Specify files

Step 4.8 – Assign files

Step 5 – Read Data

Step 5.1 – Display read data

Step 6 – Convert Data

Step 6.1 – Display converted data

Step 7 – Create batch input session

Step 8 – Run batch input session

Step 9 – Reviewing log of batch input session

Chapter 5: Common Errors

File does not exist... even if it does

Screen does not exist

Error is real and want to cancel that transaction or end it all so I can fix the file and start again

Error Code 13

Error code 7

Reproducing an error

Resources / Links

## COPYRIGHT

## NOTE FROM THE AUTHOR

*"If the people knew how hard I had to work to gain my mastery, it wouldn't seem wonderful at all."*

- *Michelangelo*

Hello there!

Firstly thank you for purchasing this book. I hope that you learn at least one new thing from here or it gets you to making your first LSMW in an hour or less.

I want to just highlight that I'm not a professional author but a professional consultant who works with LSMW on a daily basis. You can see my profile on http://linkedin.com/in/RonnieChio or simply visit my personal web portfolio www.RonnieChio.com.

The way this book has been written is as if I am right with you and talking you through things. We've done our best to review any grammatical errors, so please excuse us for any mistakes you may find.

The way this book has been strategically structured is to describe the task first then followed by a screenshot (where possible)... usually you will see something like "Per Screenshot below.... ".

Every effort has been put to making sure you have the most up to date information however please visit www.TheSAPGuy.com for the latest updates. You can also sign up to the mailing list via this website to get product updates / news.

Wish you every success moving forward!

Ronnie Chio - TheSAPGuy

*Note: The information here is not consulting advice but for the purposes for teaching you how I would operate SAP's LSMW tool.*

# ACKNOWLEDGEMENTS

There are some individuals who have contributed to writing this book. Before I get to them, I'd like to thank my wonderful wife Zoya and my children Xavier, Phoenix and Maia for being so patient and forgiving during the many hours I spent writing this book. Thank you.

I also want to take the opportunity to thanking a number of individuals who have encouraged me to writing this book or have mentored and taught me a thing or two... after all I didn't just hatch out of the egg and have this knowledge bestowed upon me.

## COLLEAGUES

To my colleagues listed below (in no specific order) - thank you for encouraging me to write this book. I know you've been saying this for years now and finally it is here.

Thank you to each of you: *Zaved Hanif, Remi Masri, Rosiana Im, Artour Kitbalian, Michael "Mike" Tarasco, Wayne Drummond, Jose Ortiz, Karen Carter, Dave Smith, Patricia Rankin, Jason Ludwig, Don Mape and Finbar Callaghan.*

## MENTORS

Throughout my working career, I've been privileged to have had the interaction with the individuals below as they have shared their knowledge and trust with me to result in what I am today. Thank you guys... let's catch up soon!

Special thanks to: *Scott Raisin, Damian Cox, George Tokitsis, Shaun Quinton, John Venetsanos, David Rose and Michael (Mick) Newton.*

# HOW TO USE THIS BOOK
**_"If you do not first empty the cup, how could you enjoy my cup of tea?"_**

**_– Bruce Lee_**

This book is designed to provide an introduction to SAP LSMW (Legacy System Migration Workbench) toolset to a wide range of readers, from SAP consultants to entry-level SAP users. As such its content is necessarily broad and not-too-technical. This book should be the first thing everyone reads about SAP LSMW tool, but will provide easy links to level 2 technical content to continue learning about various sub-topics in more detail. The contents is structured so that everyone can begin with the introduction chapter then skip to the subsequent chapters that most interest them. Experience SAP users of LSMW will likely skip to the practical application chapters while techies will jump ahead to the LSMW advance methods (tips and tricks).

The knowledge you will find in this book is the first step on the journey to becoming a super user of LSMW, but in many ways it is just the "tip of the iceberg". I am working on level 2 technical books on other LSMW methods and then furthering with LSMW application series. As the author, I am committed to providing as much application and technical content as possible through theSAPguy.com website and other channels related to theSAPguy.com. Please refer to the last chapter to get a listing of additional free information sources on LSMW.

SAP is rapidly growing its user & customer base and SAP's level of importance to SAP customers will continue to increase over the next several years. I will attempt to provide updated editions of this book on an annual basis to ensure that you can easily access the most up-to-date knowledge on SAP's LSMW toolset. Please continue to visit theSAPguy.com website to download updated and revised editions when they are released. You can also follow @theSAPguydotcom on Twitter for updates.

# CHAPTER 1: SAP LEGACY SYSTEM MIGRATION WORKBENCH (LSMW) OVERVIEW

**LSMW** – Legacy System Migration Workbench is an SAP tool that was conceived for the purpose of supporting mass migration of data. Whilst the first two letters "LS" stand for LEGACY SYSTEM, do not be fooled. LSMW was initially conceived for the purposes of transferring a customer's data from a legacy system, whether it is an older version of SAP or a totally different vendor's ERP. Nowadays, it is used for many reasons or tasks that simulate execution of a transaction with requirements to perform that very same transaction a number of times > 20 times.

Note: SAP has many products; LSMW is part of the main R/3 or ECC product and is neither used nor available for other products such as Business Intelligence Warehouse (BW/BI).

In the current version of SAP and since early R/3, LSMW supports the following standard data interface – ways for getting the data in:

- Batch input (Standard & Recording)

- Direct input

- Business Object: BAPIs (Business Application Programming Interfaces)

- IDocs (Intermediate Documents)

This tutorial helps you learn to use the LSMW using the standard interface of Batch Input via a recording.

LSMW comprises of the main functions listed below:

- A structured instruction for what LSMW is going to perform. Remember I mentioned earlier that LSMW is usually used for migrating data into SAP where a person would have to manually migrate more than 20 records. Therefore we have to somewhat "tell" LSMW what we what it to do, which transaction, what object and which fields are going to be present in our file for migration. You will see this in the 5 steps of LSMW.

- Uploading / Reading your prepared data. This is called your "Source File"

- Converting our prepared data which includes mapping a field in your spread sheet structure to the LSMW structure – known as your target field/structure.

- Final execution of the program to import into your SAP R/3 or SAP ECC system.

This tutorial is designed to be a no-nonsense or no-fluff document and as such we have created as much screen prints as possible to help you along. Make sure you keep an eye on the cursor at all times. Whilst we are only venturing into the Batch Input Recording methods, this will give you the foundation to build upon for the other methods in *theSAPGuy* series. Keep informed and sign up to our mailing list on www.theSAPGuy.com website.

## Graphical representation of LSMW process flow

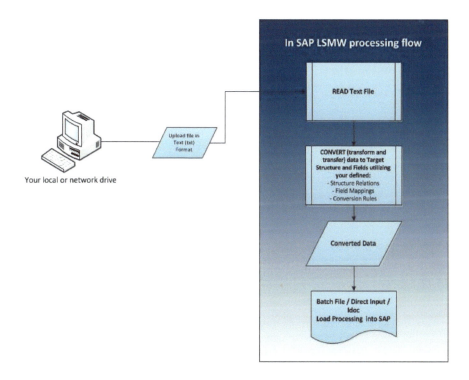

# CHAPTER 2: THREE STEPS TO FOLLOW TO MAKE A SUCCESSFUL LSMW

Yes you heard it right, we can pretty much group what we are learning here in 3 main steps.

- Know the task at hand

- Create LSMW

- Test LSMW

Read on!

## KNOW THE TASK AT HAND!

To teach you how to create an LSMW without explaining to you that you need to know the activity you want to perform is not going to be effective. Therefore I suggest that you familiarise yourself with what you are trying to do by manually creating the data yourself in the first place, even if it is unreal data – at least you will get a feel for how you want the data to look like before programmatically creating a mass migration tool in LSMW.

This is the first and most important step that will be the key to your ongoing success in migrating data and using LSMW.

## CREATE LSMW

After you have familiarized yourself with what you want to do i.e. the task at hand we then follow the steps in Chapter 4 to create our LSMW. There are a total of 14 general steps outside of the recording of which you may only need to perform 13 within this tutorial but nonetheless we will explain all 14 general steps in LSMW. Don't be fooled though, as you get more advanced in LSMW there are plenty more things you can do and you will realize the true power of LSMW. Unfortunately these advanced techniques are not in the scope of this book but in the next series of this book.

The screen print below shows the 14 general steps within the LSMW tool.

| Process Step |
| --- |
| ● Maintain Object Attributes |
| ○ Maintain Source Structures |
| ○ Maintain Source Fields |
| ○ Maintain Structure Relations |
| ○ Maintain Field Mapping and Conversion Rules |
| ○ Maintain Fixed Values, Translations, User-Defined Routines |
| ○ Specify Files |
| ○ Assign Files |
| ○ Read Data |
| ○ Display Read Data |
| ○ Convert Data |
| ○ Display Converted Data |
| ○ Create Batch Input Session |
| ○ Run Batch Input Session |

## TEST YOUR LSMW

Finally, before you go into your production system, I would suggest all of the above steps are performed in a test or training environment. Try loading more than one in your file so that you know that LSMW will work with multiple records and finally, also test different expected permutations of the task at hand i.e. sometime some fields are populated whilst other times they are completely ignored. That's it... Now let's get cracking and actually do this.

# CHAPTER 3: OVERVIEW OF WHAT WE ARE DOING – KNOWING THE TASK AT HAND.

## THE SCENARIO

In our tutorial here in the document, we will be working on the scenario that we have a number of banks that overall are referenced in our other data in order to make payment to vendors and employees. Additionally we need these banks to be created in order for us to set up a bank account to receive money.

Each bank is unique in its own way, whether we call it a SORT CODE, BSB Number or SWIFT Code with the Sort Code and so on, these banks and their specific branch can be identified using any of these codes. So the Bank of America in Time Square, New York would have a unique identifier, usually numeric and sometime alpha numeric that would differ from the Bank of America in Burlington, Vermont.

Given that any bank can be referenced multiple times by many employees using the same bank branch or your vendors / suppliers using that same bank, SAP likes to create such data as a master data. Master data is static information that gets updated only on rare occasions.

So the scenario is that we are creating bank masters. The example shown is based on creating a bank master in Brisbane Australia but the concept remains true anywhere in the world.

# CHAPTER 4: CREATING OUR FIRST LSMW

All right, let's get hands on.

## STEP 1 – ACCESSING LSMW AND THE LSMW INITIAL SCREEN

To access the LSMW transaction first you must log on to SAP and then in your command box on the top left hand corner, enter in LSMW and press your keyboard button on the green tick in the image below.

If you are succssful you should now see a heading showing: ***Legacy System Migration Workbench***

## STEP 2 – WHAT IS THIS ALL ABOUT: PROJECT, SUBPROJECT AND OBJECT

So you've been able to get to the LSMW main screen, something like shown below. The Project, Subproject and Object are a way of filing your LSMW within SAP. It is possible that you may undertake a number of projects within a system across a number of process streams. I urge you to think long term on your LSMW filing structure. For instructional purposes, I have kept this simple. Whilst there's always a way to re-structure or rename the Project, Subproject and Object naming convention it is not covered in this book specifically but will be covered in my next book – LSMW Administration which is being written as you read this book. To keep up to date with new books, updates or news simply go to www.theSAPGuy.com and register in the LOG IN page and confirm your subscription via the automated email from www.theSAPGuy.com. We will never use or sell the information you

provide us other than to communicate with you about
www.theSAPGuy.com products and latest developments.

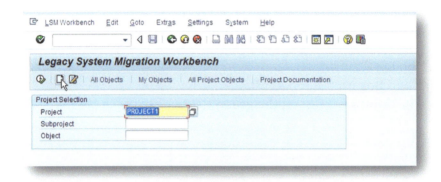

## STEP 2.1 – CREATE AN LSMW PROJECT

Let's begin, to create a project, delete all the values in the Project,
Subproject and Object fields.

At the initial screen, you can create a new project, corresponding
subprojects and objects via Edit -> Create new entry. Alternatively you
can select from an existing project

Project: An ID with a maximum of 10 characters to name your data
transfer project. If you want to transfer data from several legacy
systems, you may create a project e.g. for every legacy system

Subproject: An ID with a maximum of 10 characters that is used as
further structuring attribute

Object: An ID with a maximum of 10 characters to name the business
object

Now type the project name you'd like to use. I've used PROJECT1 as my
project name. Then click on the CREATE button looks like a blank piece
of paper shown in the next screenshot.

**19 |**

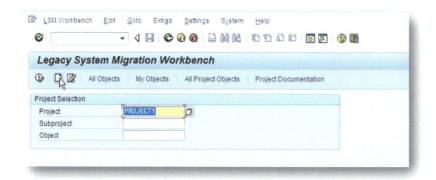

Now give your project a description, something meaning full that would tell everyone what project this is.

When done you can either press your ENTER button on the keyboard or click on the green tick / check icon.

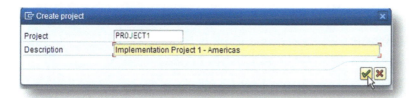

## STEP 2.2 – CREATE AN LSMW SUBPROJECT

After doing step 2.1 you will now be prompted to create a Subproject, in my example I have used "Bank_Masters" as the sub project and created a description that this Subproject may house create, update and delete LSMWs for bank masters.

When done you can either press your ENTER button on the keyboard or

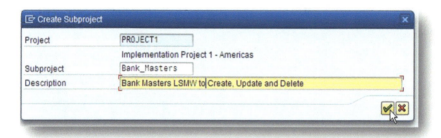

click on the green tick / check icon.

## STEP 2.3 – CREATE AN LSMW OBJECT

Finally, your object is your LSMW or activity you are doing. Imagine these as a file in Microsoft excel or Microsoft word and the first two steps were just folders and subfolders. In our example, I am performing a create bank master transaction, so for me I use the prefix "CRE" to indicate that this LSMW is a create transaction followed by what I'm doing in this instance I'm creating a bank record. The string I use ends up being CRE_BANK_RECORD and then in my Name (description) I describe this Object as an "FI01 – Create Bank Master via Recording". I've stated the transaction and also the mode by which I've created the LSMW which is recording.

When done you can either press your ENTER button on the keyboard or click on the green tick / check icon.

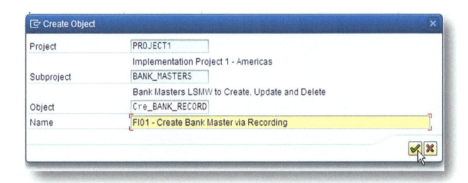

## Step 3 – Let's create our first Recording

Well done, so now you've taken care of the basic administration part of creating an LSMW, let's now create the a recording of what we want LSMW to perform repeatedly in SAP to migrate your data. You should now see the screen below if you've been successful in creating your Project, Subproject and Object. You will notice that your descriptions also displays.

To create our recording we must first go to the recording overview. Select *Go To > Recordings* or alternatively if you're like me and use the keyboard more often than the mouse, you can also get there by simply selecting *Ctrl+F2* on your keyboard.

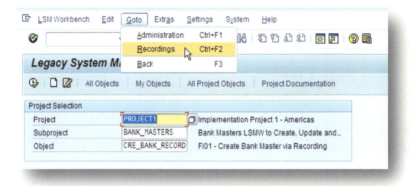

Click on the CREATE button.

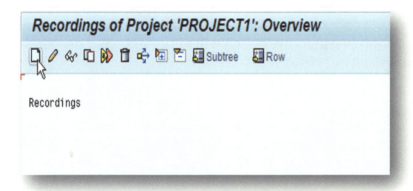

This Popup will show, create a short name for your recording. For me what I like to use is the transaction code that I'm recording, in this instance "FI01" followed by "_" and the recording version of FI01 i.e. this could be my 99th time I've recorded a different variation of transaction FI01 so I would label it "FI01_099"... seeing this is the first time we're doing this, it will be FI01_001. Like earlier, lets put some meaningful description like "Create Bank Master Record". The owner field should be automatically populated with your SAP user ID so no need to worry.

When done you can either press your ENTER button on the keyboard or click on the green tick / check icon.

It will ask you for the transaction code you want to record. Put in **FI01** and either press your ENTER button on the keyboard or click on the green tick / check icon.

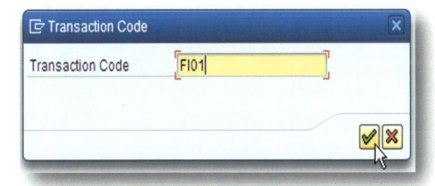

You will be taken to the screens of transaction FI01 like you were doing this manually and is recording every step of the way. Enter in the values, moving forward you can copy my screen values if you wish. Just remember if you do this a second time you may need to change the bank key. In our example below 999-001 is your bank key. If you do perform this again, you may need to use one that does not exist in your system or have not been used in your file / recording.

When done you can either press your ENTER button on the keyboard or click on the green tick / check icon.

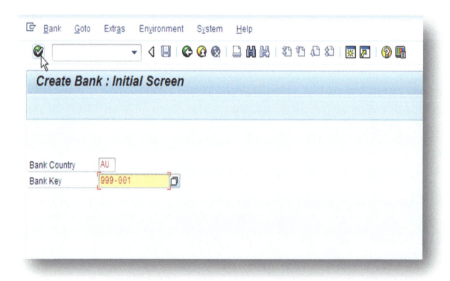

Populate the screen with your desired details or use my screenshot details. If a similar record exists, a popup may display you can just ENTER your way past that popup or adjust your values.

When done you can either press your ENTER button on the keyboard or click on the green tick / check icon.

After entering in all the details per above, click on the save button  or press Ctrl+S.

Congratulations, you have just created your first Recording in LSMW. You should now see the screen below.

As you can see, the values you used during the recording is also show in the next screenshot followed by pink fields.

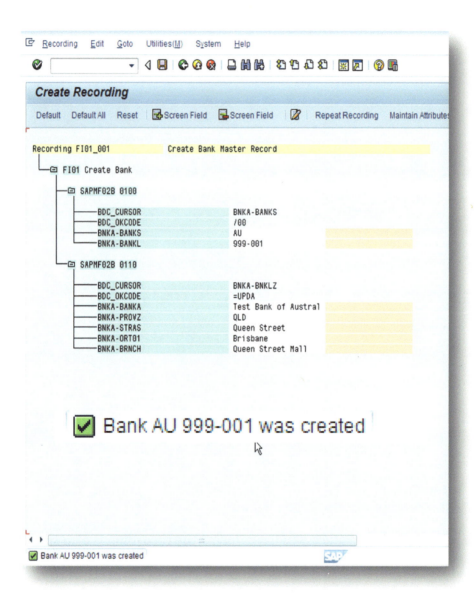

Next we will automatically allow SAP to generate the field names and descriptions using the internal SAP dictionary. Simply click on "Default All" button as shown below.

You should now see that your screen should look like below with the pink section having the SAP technical name and next to it is the description.

Important thing to note... the tables that are being affected for each field are shown in the blue section on the left of the values you inputed in the recording. In this example is BNKA-BANKA (the BNKA is the table and the BANKA after the dash is the technical name for the "Name of Bank" field.

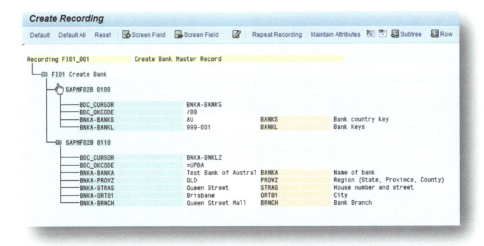

What we need to do next is to remove the values we originally entered to create the recording as if you don't, your LSMW will automatically assume that when your file is blank or not populated then the values in this field becomes the substitute/default value.

To do this, simply double click on the values you wish to delete and under the Default Value field you can delete the entry in there and leave it blank. (See below). Do this for every field that you don't want a default value for.

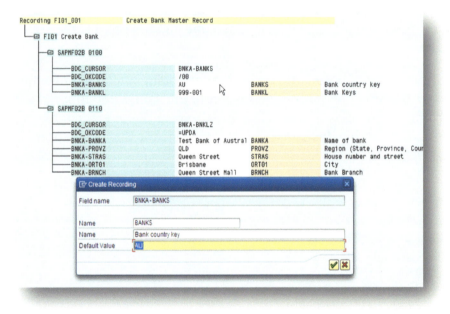

At then end of this exercise you will then see the screen on the next page.

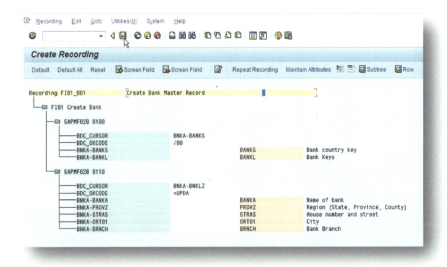

## STEP 3.1 – DOWNLOAD THE RECORDING

What we need to do next is to download the recording. This exercise is not only useful when you have multiple SAP environments to utilize your recording. The purpose for this exercise is in the context of creating a file template for your LSMW and also to streamline a few steps in LSMW.

Follow the path on the next screenshot.

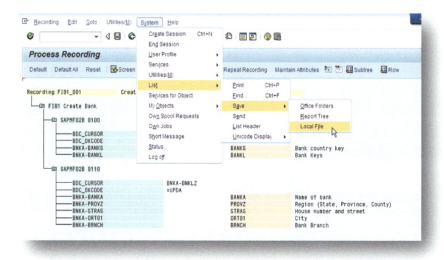

You will then get a popup screen. Follow the next screenshots and will transpire sequentially as shown.

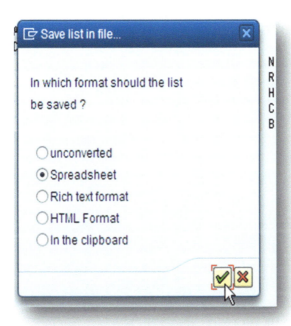

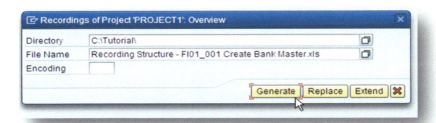

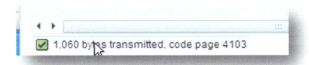

When you get the message shown previously, this confirms you have downloaded the recording correctly.

STEP 3.2 – PREPARATION FOR FAST TRACKING LATER STEPS

*"If I had eight hours to chop down a tree, I'd spend six sharpening my axe"*

*- Abrahm Lincoln*

I'm a big believer in not wasting time and also preparation. Just like those chefs you see on the cooking shows where the perform a lot of preparation before cooking, we should also take note and prepare where possible. Think through the steps before actioning.

The next steps transpire in Microsoft Excel or an equivalent program. The screenshots below are captured using Microsoft Excel 2007.

First step is to open Microsoft Excel then select the File > Open in your menu bar. You will need to direct to the folder where you saved the recording and follow the steps shown in the next few screenshots.

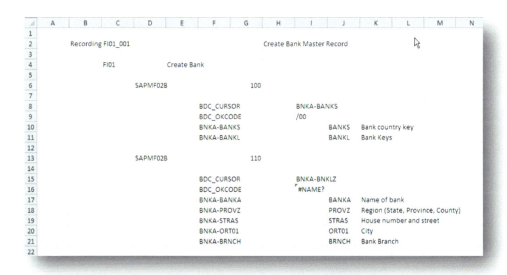

If you see the previous screenshot you will notice that your recording is now in the excel format. The two most important columns are J & K. We can delete all other columns other than J & K and delete any rows that are blank after this. Finally insert 2 columns in between the two columns remaining and your file should look like below.

| | A | B | C | D | E | F | G |
|---|---|---|---|---|---|---|---|
| 1 | BANKS | | | Bank country key | | | |
| 2 | BANKL | | | Bank Keys | | | |
| 3 | BANKA | | | Name of bank | | | |
| 4 | PROVZ | | | Region (State, Province, County) | | | |
| 5 | STRAS | | | House number and street | | | |
| 6 | ORT01 | | | City | | | |
| 7 | BRNCH | | | Bank Branch | | | |
| 8 | | | | | | | |

The next steps are rather advanced and has some advanced SAP user features and is not in the context of this book. Therefore, I will not be providing indepth background on what every step is about but only to show you the next activities that will need to take place.

The first thing is to go to your main screen by hitting back until you go back to the first SAP screen or you can create a new session (SAP screen) and follow the steps below.

Go to transaction SE11 via your command bar.

By default the Database table has been selected. Type in table BNKA. Refer to previous paragraph to understand BNKA here.

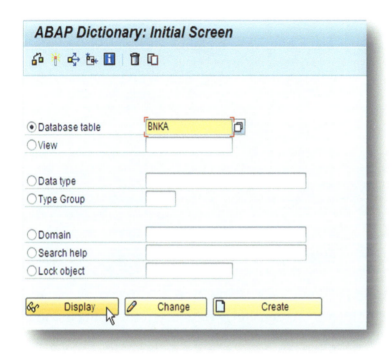

In the next screenshot, you will see that there's a list of Field names and their Lengths... this is what we're after. If you see a value in the decimal column simply add the Length value + the decimal value and then 1 (for the decimal) to get your source field value.

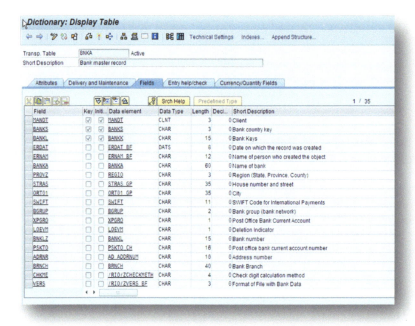

As shown in the next screenshot, I've selected the fields found in your recording. You can see the recording here.

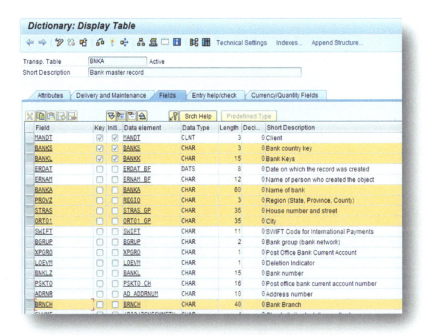

In your spreadsheet we want you to look that the field lengths in SAP and then populate them against the row that has the same field name. You will soon see why we do this... for now simply do this.

Well done, we will use this later.

STEP 3.3 – CREATING & POPULATING YOUR TEMPLATE

Now that we have an excel spreadsheet with your load structure. We will start leveraging that can create a template then populate it for LSMW use.

First step is to select all the technical fields in column A and copy.

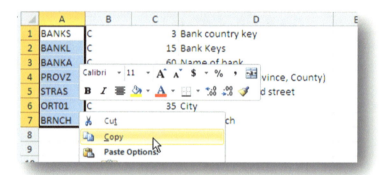

Create a new sheet or workbook (excel file) and select cell A1 then follow the screens below.

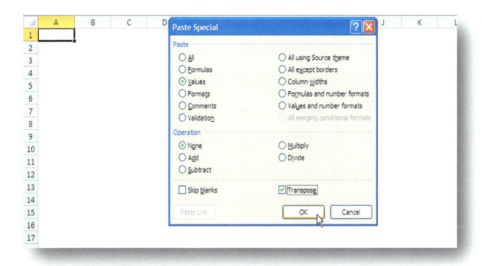

You now have a spreadsheet with column headings.

Now if you remember how we created the data in early chapters, simply populate the template with your data that you want to load. See next image as an example.

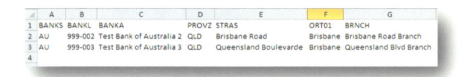

Here's a little advice, when working with Excel and saving things as a text format, Excel will automatically do some encoding in the text file so that it knows when you open it where the separator is and opens your files in columns. So when you have a comma, double quote or a character in your file, it's best to do a find and replace before saving your data i.e. Find " and Replace with something ridiculous that would never show up in the file for migration like THESAPGUY.

Then once you save your file and close it, open the file in wordpad or notepad and find and replace " with nothing (literally put no value in the replace with field) and finally find and replace THESAPGUY with " so as to re-instate where the double quotes should be in your file.

Save the file as UniCode Text just in case your SAP system is unicode compliant. Follow the screenshots below.

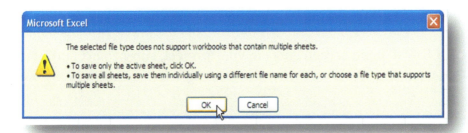

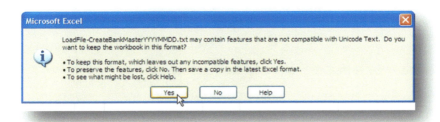

Congratulations you now have a load file.

## STEP 4 – PUTTING IT TOGETHER

So far, we have done 3 major steps

1. We have created a recording on one hand which is what we want LSMW to perform repeatedly.

2. We have created have created a template and sample data for our testing.

3. We have sourced field lengths for future use in the next steps.

Now let's begin by going back to the LSMW main screen. Simply follow the steps below. Notes will only be created where further explanation is required.

STEP 4.1 – MAINTAIN OBJECT ATTRIBUTES

In your LSMW main screen enter in your project, sub-project and Object name.

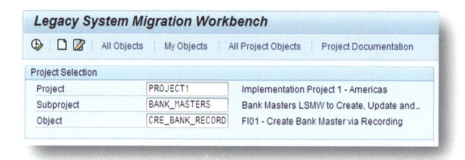

Click Execute and this will take you into the nuts and bolts of your LSMW.

You should see the available process steps (below). This is the nuts and volts that make your LSMW.

Some quick housekeeping:

Select the "Double Click" button and it will toggle to Display or Change. This simply means when you double click on to a step you will automatically be transferred in the Change or Display mode of that step. I like to have Double Click = Change.

Secondly, it's also sometimes useful if you click on numbering on so that you can clearly see how the steps you must do and what steps you're up to. For the purposes of this book we will have this turned on. Again this option will toggle between On and Off depending on what setting you have. See next image for illustration.

Your screen should now have numbers against the steps per below.

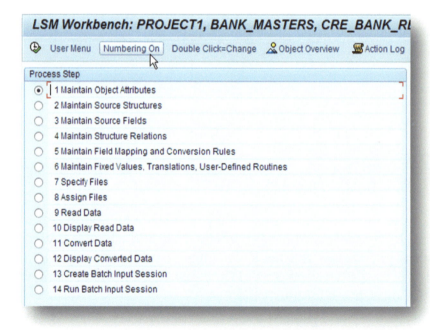

Next we ensure we do this step by step so step has already been selected therefore we will just click on execute.

Now you will see the LSMW attributes.. here you can change the description of the LSMW.

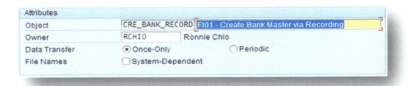

Now populate your screen below by selecting the "Batch Input Recording" node and then in the Recording field you can type in or drop down and select or if the last LSMW recording you created is the one you used simply press space bar and it should remember and give you that recording name automatically.

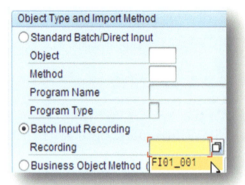

Once your screen looks like the next screenshot, simply save by clicking on save button or like in Microsoft products you can use Control + S

Save Button

Now go back to LSMW process steps menu. This is a repetitive step over and over again after the save button.

## STEP 4.2 – MAINTAIN SOURCE STRUCTURES

Here we are defining the structure of our source file. There are cases when there is a parent and child relationship and you have multiple files. In our example we will only create a single structure.

Execute Step 2 Maintain Source Structures.

You should see the screen below. Simply select the words "Source Structures" and then click on the New button (looks like the white paper in the next screenshot).

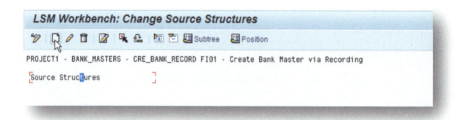

You will get the pop up screen and you will need to populate the Source Structure – A short meaning full name for your structure. No SPACES allowed so I've used underscores "_" to represent spaces.

Also add a meaning full description of your structure. Then press enter or click on the green check.

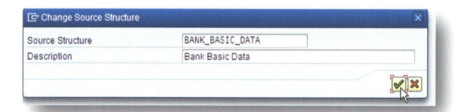

You should now see the structure in the next page. If you want to add other structures, simply create on the parent structure you want to add either an equal or child level to by clicking new you will get that option. What we've really done here is create a structure to represent our file. Now Save and go back.

## STEP 4.3 – MAINTAIN SOURCE FIELDS

Now that we have our source structure (representative of how many text files we have) we must define in LSMW what our file looks like i.e. the columsn in the file, what they mean, the type of records they are and length of that field that should be migrated.

Now seeing we did some good work earlier, go back to your spreadsheet that looks like below and select the entire data section and copy.

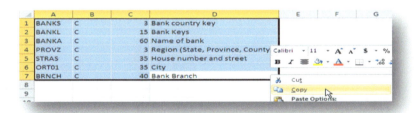

Now go back to SAP and in your LSMW processing steps select step 3 Maintain Source Fields and execute.

Now Select the structure we just created in the previous step.

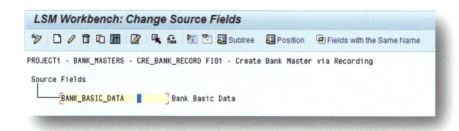

Click on the button shown below which is a fast way to enter or create fields to represent the columns in your spreadsheet.

You should now see the next screen and simply press Control + V (paste).

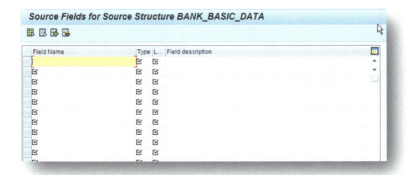

Your screen should look like below. You've just saved yourself a whole load of typing by following through this book step by step. You can now get rid of that spreadsheet if you like.

Go back one screen.

*Source Fields for Source Structure BANK_BASIC_DATA*

| Field Name | Type | L... | Field description |
|---|---|---|---|
| BANKS | C | 3 | Bank country key |
| BANKL | C | 15 | Bank Keys |
| BANKA | C | 60 | Name of bank |
| PROVZ | C | 3 | Region (State, Province, County) |
| STRAS | C | 35 | House number and street |
| ORT01 | C | 35 | City |
| BRNCH | C | 40 | Bank Branch |

Your screen should show like below. Save and go back to LSMW processing steps screen.

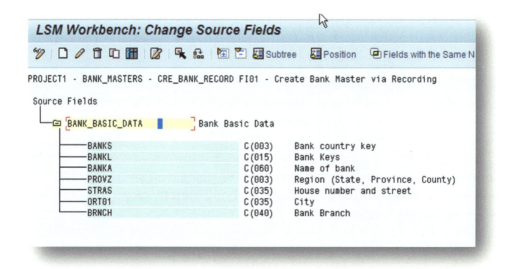

## STEP 4.4 – MAINTAIN STRUCTURE RELATIONS

Well done. So far you have:

- Created a recording;

- Created an LSMW;

- Referenced the recording in essence telling the LSMW what it will be doing;

-  Created a structure that represents each of your file (one file = one structure) and their relationship to each other in reference to what you want to do in the recording.

- Defined the columns in your recording in the order of your template with the length and types. I've used "C" for character and is usually good for almost everything.

Now we do the next step. Select step 4 Maintain Structure Relations and execute.

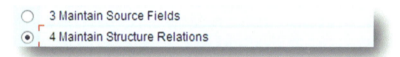

What we are really doing here is pointing your source structure (files) to the structure of your recording . When you learn more advance or alternative ways of creating an LSMW you may see the need to have mutliple structures but in our example you will find that SAP recognises you only have 1 structure in your recording and 1 structure in your source so it automatically assigns these to each other.

Click Save and Back.

### Step 4.5 – Maintain field mapping and conversion rules

So far, you have now told LSMW exactly what you want it to do in your recording and told it what your file looks like. Then in the previous step you assigned each source (text file) and target structures (recording) to each other.

Now we assigning source fields to your target field structures so SAP knows which column in your file should populate the SAP fields you recorded. Select step 5 - Maintain Field Mapping and Conversion Rules and execute.

Now given that this is intended to be a beginners guide, I'm not going through the advanced techniques for mapping and converting the data. You can find that in my series of publications either Kindle Singles or www.theSAPguy.com or www.RonnieChio.com.

You should be at the screen shown in the next page.

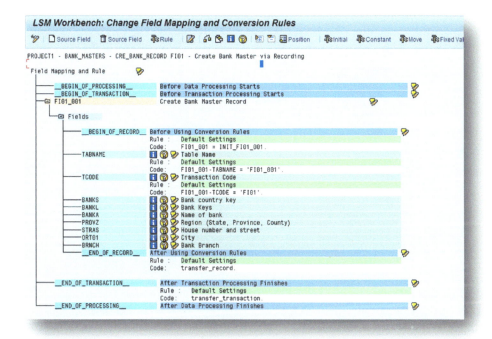

Now follow the screenshot below.

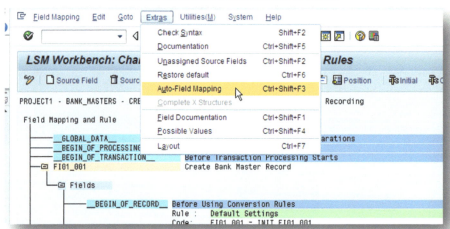

You will get a popup shown below. Simply populate the popup like below.

What you are really doing here is automatically mapping the fields between source and target structures. This only works if you have exactly the same names. This is why I asked you to download your recording and create a file. Play with these settings to see different results then press ENTER when done.

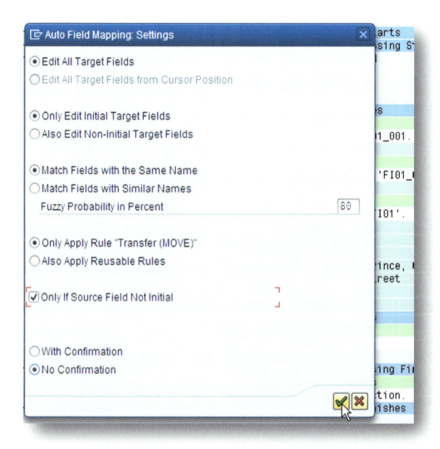

You should get a confirmation like shown below when done.

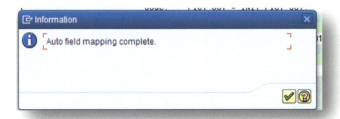

You should now see that your BANKS is mapped to BANKS source field in the source structure that you created. You'll also see a code created for you showing: If not Source Structure + Source field is initial – this means as long as your file value for that records/row is not blank it will then do then next part of the code which simply states that Target field BANKS = Source Field BANKS and so on.

This technique will save you heaps of time specially when you sometimes have a long list of source and target fields to map.

PROJECT1 - BANK_MASTERS - CRE_BANK_RECORD FI01 - Create Bank Master via Recording

## STEP 4.6 – QUICK OVERVIEW OF FIXED VALUES, TRANSLATIONS AND USER-DEFINED ROUTINES

The next processing step we are not going to perform but you can play with it. Simply put, Step 6 Maintain Fixed Values, Translation, User-Defined routines are advance transformation capability in LSMW.

In each of these you can create a predefine value and reuse it between LSMWs in the same project.

Maintain Fixed Values this is where you could alias a word to always mean the same thing and use it within your LSMW field mapping to always equal that value. You may create a fixed value called 'zActive' that always has a fixed value of 'X' so whenever you reference the zActive in your code, the LSMW always knows that you want it to put an 'X' there.

Translation is where your source file has a particular character or word like 'China' and you always want to enter it in SAP as 'CN'. So here you can transform your data without having to do it earlier in Excel and again this is reusable.

User-Defined routines are where you can really get funky and advanced in LSMW. This is where you can start writing checks against SAP configuration.

I will be shortly publishing more tutorials on this and can be downloaded from my websites www.theSAPguy.com or www.RonnieChio.com. Alternatively you can also get these as Kindle singles via www.Amazon.com.

STEP 4.7 – SPECIFY FILES

Remember we created source structures to represent each file? Well this is where we tell the LSMW which files and their file path we will be using for this LSMW. Select step 7 Specify Files and Execute.

Double click on the word "Legacy Data" per next screenshot.

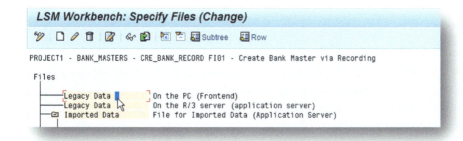

Popup will show per below. Now using the button on the cursor simply navidaget o the file/s you want to use for the LSMW and give it a name that is meaningful.

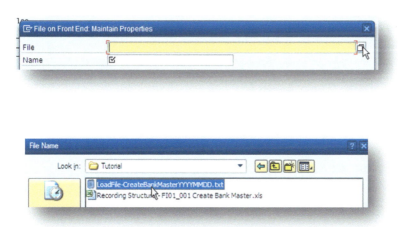

Now finalise your screen by ensuring it looks like the next screenshot and click/press ENTER key. The nodes are self explanatory so I didn't go through much detail here.

Now when you see the following screen you can click Save and Back to the Processing steps menu.

```
Files
    ─⊞ Legacy Data          On the PC (Frontend)
        └─File to Create Bank Basic Data C:\Tutorial\LoadFile-CreateBankMasterYYYYMMDD.txt
                             Data for One Source Structure (Table)
                             Separator Tabulator
                             Field Names at Start of File
                             Field Order Matches Source Structure Definition
                             With Record End Indicator (Text File)
                             Code Page ASCII
    ─ Legacy Data           On the R/3 server (application server)
    ─⊞ Imported Data         File for Imported Data (Application Server)
        └─Imported Data              PROJECT1_BANK_MASTERS_CRE_BANK_RECORD.1smw.read
    ─⊞ Converted Data        File for Converted Data (Application Server)
        └─Converted Data             PROJECT1_BANK_MASTERS_CRE_BANK_RECORD.1smw.conv
    └─Wildcard Value         Value for Wildcard '*' in File Name
```

You may get an error like below. So simply follow the next steps to counter this error.

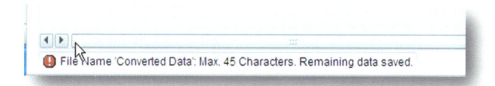

Double click on the value of "Converted Data" and reduce this from the left (NOT the right) so that you have less than 45 charaters in all then press/click Enter. Save and go back again to LSMW processing steps screen. These steps are demonstrated in the next few images.

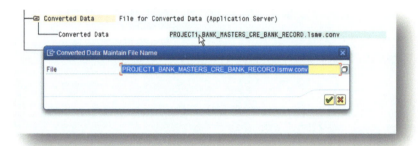

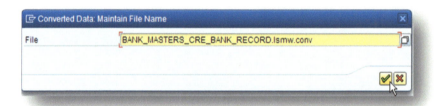

## STEP 4.8 – ASSIGN FILES

So after step 4.7- specify files, now we have to allocate the list of files we have referenced in that step to the source structure. We are in effect marrying the source structure to a file that we have referenced to be used in this LSMW.

Select Step 8 Assign Files and Execute

Where you have specified multiple files, you must select the structure you want to start assigning files to and click Assign and then select your file. However in our example, given we have one source structure and one source file this is recognized by SAP and already done for us. Click Save and go Back.

```
PROJECT1 - BANK_MASTERS - CRE_BANK_RECORD FI01 - Create Bank Master via Recording

Source Structures and Files

    BANK_BASIC_DATA Bank Basic Data
                    File to Create Bank Basic Data C:\Tutorial\LoadFile-CreateBankMasterYYYYMMDD.txt
```

## STEP 5 – READ DATA

Now this is where the execution steps begin. So far we have completed the LSMW and in essence added the meat to the skeletons. Now let's see if our LSMW does what it's suppose to do.

Select step 9 Read Data and Execute

You will be confronted with the screen per below. Here you have the option to select which line in your file we will be reading by entering in the from and to with the line number range. Given in our Specify File step we selected that there is column headings, this LSMW automatically ignores Row 1 of your file (the heading) and begins from Row 2.

I generally leave this blank.

Now you have two other options available on this screen.

- Value Fields -> 1234.56

This setting is important when you have target fields that require values to be in the number format. On read it will automatically identify the source field value for number foramt target field to be 1234.56 format.

- Date Value -> YYYYMMDD

This setting is important when you have target fields that require the dates to be in the YYYYMMDD format and your file currently has DDMMYYYY. On read it will automatically rearrange the source field value for date target field to be YYYYMMDD.

For the purpose of our exercise and this book we will leave things as they are and Execute.

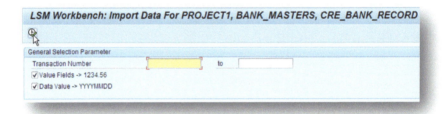

On execute it will do a record count of how many records in the file and how many records "Read" or picked up in the file and saved in SAP repository. It will look like the next screen. When you are satisfied it has the correct data count per your file (exclude heading if you have one) then hit back until you get to the processing step screen.

| File(s) Read: | C:\Tutorial\LoadFile-CreateBankMasterYYYYMMDD.txt | | |
|---|---|---|---|
| File Written: | PROJECT1_BANK_MASTERS_CRE_BANK_RECORD.1smw.read | | |
| Source Structure | Read | Written | Not Written |
| BANK_BASIC_DATA | 2 | 2 | 0 |
| Transactions Read: | 2 | | |
| Records Read: | 2 | | |
| Transactions Written: | 2 | | |
| Records Written: | 2 | | |

## STEP 5.1 – DISPLAY READ DATA

This processing step is simply an opportunity for you to review ("eye ball") that your data that's been read has been read correctly by the LSMW and is populated in the correct source fields. If you find anything wrong you must go to either "Field Mapping" step or "Specify Files" step. Follow the next few screenshots and the cursors.

○ 9 Read Data
◉ 10 Display Read Data

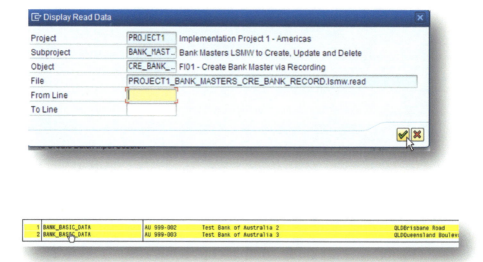

To review the data in their source fields simply double click on one of the yellow lines (per above screenshot) and then you will see a vertical detailed representation of your data in your source fields / structures.

Once happy that all data seems to be allocated in the correct structure, simply hit SAVE and go Back to processing steps.

| File | PROJECT1_BANK_MASTERS_CRE_BANK_RECORD.1smw.read | |
|---|---|---|
| Structure | BANK_BASIC_DATA | |
| Field Name | Field Text | Field Value |
| BANKS | Bank country key | AU |
| BANKL | Bank Keys | 999-002 |
| BANKA | Name of bank | Test Bank of Australia 2 |
| PROVZ | Region (State, Province, County) | QLD |
| STRAS | House number and street | Brisbane Road |
| ORT01 | City | Brisbane |
| BRNCH | Bank Branch | Brisbane Road Branch |

## STEP 6 – CONVERT DATA

The next step is intended to perform any transformations that you have specified in the field mapping and then sending that result into the target structures/fields.

I will not go through this in detail as it is exactly the same step as Step 5 Read Data. You can follow along with the screenshots.

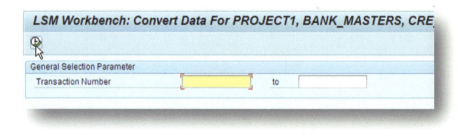

```
File Read:          PROJECT1_BANK_MASTERS_CRE_BANK_RECORD.1smw.read
File Written:       BANK_MASTERS_CRE_BANK_RECORD.1smw.conv

Transactions Read:          2
Records Read:               2
Transactions Written:       2
Records Written:            2
```

## STEP 6.1 – DISPLAY CONVERTED DATA

This step is similar to Step 5.1 Display Read Data therefore I will not duplicate the instructions but simply know that in this step you will see the result of Step 6 Convert Data in their respective target fields.

○  11 Convert Data
⦿  12 Display Converted Data

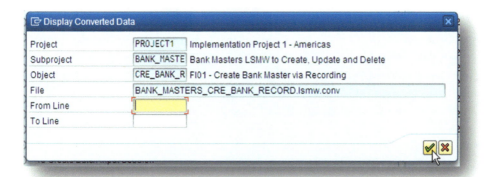

| ☞ Display Converted Data | | | |
|---|---|---|---|
| Project | PROJECT1 | Implementation Project 1 - Americas | |
| Subproject | BANK_MASTE | Bank Masters LSMW to Create, Update and Delete | |
| Object | CRE_BANK_R | FI01 - Create Bank Master via Recording | |
| File | BANK_MASTERS_CRE_BANK_RECORD.lsmw.conv | | |
| From Line | | | |
| To Line | | | |

| Row | Struct. | Contents | | | |
|---|---|---|---|---|---|
| 1 | FI01_001 | FI01_001 | FI01 | AU 999-002 | Test Bank of Australia 2 |
| 2 | FI01_001 | FI01_001 | FI01 | AU 999-003 | Test Bank of Australia 3 |

File BANK_MASTERS_CRE_BANK_RECORD.lsmw.conv

Structure FI01_001

| Fld Name | Fld Text | FldValue |
|---|---|---|
| TABNAME | Table Name | FI01_001 |
| TCODE | Transaction Code | FI01 |
| BANKS | Bank country key | AU |
| BANKL | Bank Keys | 999-003 |
| BANKA | Name of bank | Test Bank of Australia 3 |
| PROVZ | Region (State, Province, County) | QLD |
| STRAS | House number and street | Queensland Boulevarde |
| ORT01 | City | Brisbane |
| BRNCH | Bank Branch | Queensland Blvd Branch |

STEP 7 – CREATE BATCH INPUT SESSION

Now that we've gone through converting the data, we will now prepare a batch file – think of this as a file within SAP in the format that it requires to process and load data into SAP.

Select step 13 - Create Batch Input Session and Execute.

○  12 Display Converted Data

◉  13 Create Batch Input Session

There's nothing to enter here so simply Execute again.

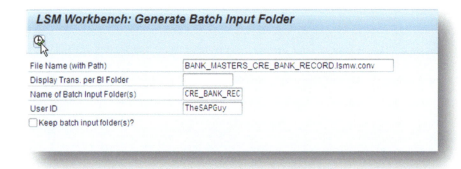

Now it should give you a confirmation like below stating that 1 file was created with 2 records (paraphrasing here).

If the counts add up to your intended volume of data for migration then simply press/Click enter and go back to processing steps menu.

## STEP 8 – RUN BATCH INPUT SESSION

This is the step we've all been working towards... time to upload and migrate your data.

Select Step 14 Run Batch Input Session.

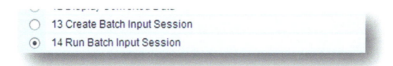

You should now automatically be directed to your file. Another way to get here is via transaction SM35 but lets keep it simple.

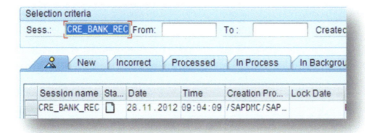

Now select the file you want to execute by clicking on the left node representing the Session name you want to run and click on Execute.

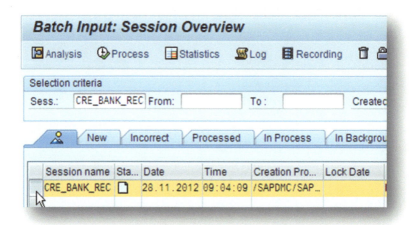

You will be asked for some options in which you want to run your file. Your options are

- Process/foreground: This is the slowest possible way for migrating but is a good way to debug or understand where your errors are. This processing method will stop at every recording screen and move on until you press enter on your keyboard.

- Display errors only: This processing method is a hybrid of the foreground and background. What it does is process your upload in the background which means you don't have to press enter at every screen in your LSMW recording but it stops when it hits and error or invalid field value. This gives you an option on error to move forward with the command "/n" on your command window or completely stopping by entering in "/nend" or "/bend".

- Background: This is the fastest way to load your data. What this does is process all records and on error it will skip that record and move to the next one.

All of these processing modes will produce an error log. We'll go through the error log in the next chapter.

For now make sure your settings are like below and click on process.

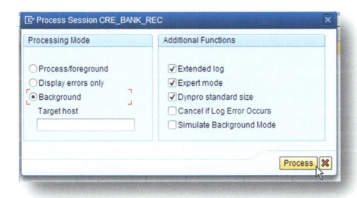

When you've successfully executed you will receive the same message below in your status bar.

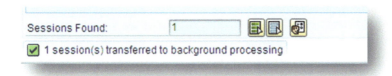

If you are successful in your load, you should not have any batch files in the batch input session overview.

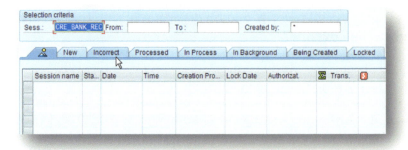

Congratulations! You have loaded.

STEP 9 – REVIEWING LOG OF BATCH INPUT SESSION

If you want to see the log of your load simply click on the Log button per below.

Select the session. It is possible to have multiple sessions for your load if you have executed lots of files for the same LSMW or the same batch files more than once until your load is 100% successful.

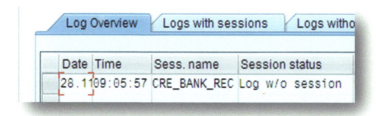

Click on display button

You should now see a log of everything that transpired in your session followed by a count.

| Time | Message |
|------|---------|
| 09:05:57 | Session CRE_BANK_REC is being processed by user |
| 09:05:57 | Bank AU 999-002 was created |
| 09:05:57 | Transaction was processed successfully |
| 09:05:57 | Bank AU 999-003 was created |
| 09:05:57 | Transaction was processed successfully |
| 09:05:57 | Batch input session deleted |
| 09:05:57 | Processing statistics |
| 09:05:57 | 2 transactions read |
| 09:05:57 | 2 transactions processed |
| 09:05:57 | 0 transactions with errors |
| 09:05:57 | 0 transactions deleted |
| 09:05:57 | Batch input processing ended |

# CHAPTER 5: COMMON ERRORS

I've put together some common errors that I encountered when I was learning LSMW.

### FILE DOES NOT EXIST... EVEN IF IT DOES

If you ever get this message, it's actually a simple one. The file path and file name combined is too long. This happens when you've got either many layers of folders to get to the file or the file name is really long.

I suggest you create a folder directly in your C:\ root directory so that the path looks like C:\<folder name>\<filename.txt>

You can then re-file it however you like but when processing in LSMW this is a simple way of avoiding this problem in the first place.

### SCREEN DOES NOT EXIST

This can sometime happen if there are pop-ups that you haven't recorded or the screen in SAP changes depending on a field value.

Whilst it may not always result in success - if you run Chapter 4 Step 8 in "Display Errors Mode Only" processing method, you will be able to process the record by holding down the enter button with something heavy.

I've worked with many consultants and I've seen it all... from a lucky 10 cent coin jammed in between the enter button to balancing mobile phones to keep the enter button down. Use whatever you like but you must keep the enter button down.

### ERROR IS REAL AND WANT TO CANCEL THAT TRANSACTION OR END IT ALL SO I CAN FIX THE FILE AND START AGAIN

If you are running in "Process/Foreground" or "Display Errors Mode Only" processing method and it happens that you encounter an error that is blatantly wrong in your text file then you can do one of the two options:

- To pass that particular record being migrated and moving on to the next one, simply enter /n in the pop-up command box.

- To end the execution of the batch file, simply enter /nend or /bend in the pop-up command box.

## ERROR CODE 13

This error simply means that the file you are trying to upload in the "Read Data" step is open in another program. Close it and re-execute the "Read Data" step.

## ERROR CODE 7

This error simply means that setting within the "Specify file" step is set incorrectly.

Go back to Specify Files step 4.7 and make sure in the Code Page section that ASCII is selected.

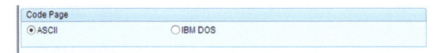

## REPRODUCING AN ERROR

Whilst it may not always result in success - if you run Chapter 4 Step 8 in "Process/Foreground" processing method, you will be able to process the record and step through every screen. Simply press enter to move to the next screen.

Using this method, if you have a handful of records that have a small anomaly you can override the value being pushed from your file with your own by simply entering your desired field value.

# Author's Closing Note

Well done! That is all to it for this particular method of creating an LSMW. This is probably the easiest way but definitely not the most efficient way.

This book is to introduce and familiarize you with this tool that SAP has created. I am already writing a book on the other methods using Standard Batch / Direct input programs, IDocs and BAPI via LSMW. There are a lot of information that I'll be writing about shortly including creating your own advance translation and validations functions within LSMW with output reports.

To keep in the loop when these new books come out, sign up to our mailing list.

Finally, as I mentioned before, I am not a professional author but an SAP consultant. My wife and I run a boutique SAP consulting firm.

You can visit our corporate website on www.WCMGglobal.com or www.WCMGglobal.com.au.

If you have any useful suggestions, please drop us a line in contact us page on www.TheSAPGuy.com.

Lastly, I've listed out some of the links I've referenced throughout this book in the last section on the next page.

Again thank you for taking the time to read and buy this book. This book has not been created as a "For Profit" project and will be donating proceeds to charitable causes. I'll let you all know via the websites what the proceeds have been distributed.

# Resources / Links

**Author's professional web based portfolio:**

www.RonnieChio.com

**LinkedIn profile:**

http://linkedin.com/in/RonnieChio

**Twitter:**

https://twitter.com/TheSAPGuydotcom

*(D'OH! someone's taken TheSAPGuy)*

**Updates, additional resources and other products:**

www.TheSAPGuy.com

**Consulting practice:**

www.WCMGglobal.com OR www.WCMGglobal.com.au

www.ingramcontent.com/pod-product-compliance
Lightning Source LLC
Chambersburg PA
CBHW041143050326
40689CB00001B/468